Published in the UK by Bible Reading Fellowship
15 The Chambers, Vineyard, Abingdon, Oxfordshire, OX14 3FE, UK
ISBN 978-1-84101-597-2

First edition 2008

Copyright © 2008 Anno Domini Publishing
1 Churchgates, The Wilderness, Berkhamsted, Herts HP4 2UB
Text copyright © 2008 Anno Domini Publishing
Illustrations copyright © 2008 Maria Cristina lo Cascio

Publishing Director Annette Reynolds
Editor Nicola Bull
Art Director Gerald Rogers
Pre-production Krystyna Kowalska Hewitt
Production John Laister

Scripture quotations are taken from the Contemporary English Version of the Bible, published by
HarperCollins Publishers, copyright © 1991, 1992, 1995 American Bible Society.

The prayers on pages 12 and 58 are inspired by and adapted from
Common Worship: Services and Prayers for the Church of England
(Church House Publishing, 2000) copyright © The Archbishops' Council 2000

The prayer on page 58 is from
The Methodist Worship Book © Trustees for Methodist Church Purposes.
Used by permission of the Methodist Publishing House.

All rights reserved

Printed and bound in Malaysia

My Special
BABY BOOK

Sally Ann Wright

Illustrated by

Maria Cristina lo Cascio

In the Beginning

You have looked deep into my heart, LORD,
and you know all about me.
You notice everything I do; protect me and keep me safe.
You put me together inside my mother's body,
you formed me in my mother's womb.
You know every bone in my body; you know exactly how I was made.
You watched me grow from conception to birth;
all the stages of my life were spread out before you,
the days of my life all prepared before I'd even lived one day.
I praise you because of the wonderful way you created me.
Lead me in the ways of truth, dear Lord,
and guide me on the road to eternal life.

Based on Psalm 139

Scan date
_____

Scan photo

A New Baby

My name

My date of birth

The time I was born

Where I was born

My weight

The colour of my eyes

The colour of my hair

Children are a blessing and a gift from the Lord.
Psalm 127:3

Father God, creator of all that is good,
this new baby fills us with wonder and awe.
Thank you for giving us this precious new life
to nurture and protect.
Give us strength through all the joys and struggles ahead
to love and care for our new baby, this special gift from you.

This is my hand print

A New Baby
Use these two pages for your own photographs

Thanksgiving for the Gift of a Child

Thank you, Father God,
for the safe delivery of this new baby,
for the wonder of new life
and for the mystery of human love.
Thank you that you know each of us by name
and loved us even before we were born.
Help us as we learn the joys and challenges of parenthood,
to live one day at a time
and to trust you to provide for us
as each new need arises.

Thank you, Father,
that you give good things to your children,
to those who love you.
Help us, like you,
to give only good things
to this child, this new person,
this gift of life.

Where my Thanksgiving Service was held

The date of my Thanksgiving Service

The people who were there with me

Jesus said, 'Be kind to each of these little ones, for their angels in heaven always see the face of my Father in heaven.'

Based on Matthew 18:10

My Great Grandfather's name

_____

Where born

_____

When born

_____

My Great Grandmother's name

_____

Where born

_____

When born

_____

My Great Grandfather's name

_____

Where born

_____

When born

_____

My Great Grandmother's name

_____

Where born

_____

When born

_____

My Grandfather's name

_____

Where born

_____

When born

_____

My Grandmother's name

_____

Where born

_____

When born

_____

My Father's name

_____

Where born

_____

When born

_____

My Father's Family
Use these two pages for your own photographs

My Great Grandfather's name

_____

Where born

_____

When born

_____

My Great Grandmother's name

_____

Where born

_____

When born

_____

My Great Grandfather's name

_____

Where born

_____

When born

_____

My Great Grandmother's name

_____

Where born

_____

When born

_____

My Grandfather's name

_____

Where born

_____

When born

_____

My Grandmother's name

_____

Where born

_____

When born

_____

My Mother's name

_____

Where born

_____

When born

_____

My Mother's Family
Use these two pages for your own photographs

My Family

Thank you, Lord, for brothers and sisters,
thank you for the gift of my family.
Thank you that you are here with us,
that your love surrounds us,
and that you have given us each other to care for,
learn from and share with, day by day.

Name

_____

Date of birth

_____

Name

_____

Date of birth

_____

Name

_____

Date of birth

_____

Name

_____

Date of birth

_____

My Family
Use these two pages for your own photographs

My Home

Home address

_____

_____

_____

_____

Lord Jesus,
you shared in Nazareth the life of an earthly home.
Bless our home now with peace and joy.
Give to parents strength and wisdom
as the sun rises each morning,
love and patience to get through each day,
and peaceful rest as the stars light up the night sky.

Lord God,

you made the world and it was very good.

Lord God,

you gave me a home,

a place where I can be safe from harm.

Lord God,

you gave me people to love me and care for me.

Thank you for all the good things

you have given me.

What my room looks like

_____

_____

_____

_____

_____

My Progress

Date of my first smile

_____

Date of my first tooth

_____

I first slept through the night on

_____

Lord, bless us and protect us.
Lord, smile on us and show us your love.
Lord, take care of us and help us.

My Progress

Use these two pages for your own photographs

My Progress

I first sat up unaided

I first crawled

My first words

My first steps

My first immunisation

_____

My first dry night

_____

My first...

_____

Jesus, friend of little children,
be a friend to me;
take my hand, and ever keep me
close to thee.
Walter J. Matham (1853–1931)

My Progress

Use these two pages for your own photographs

My Special Things

Special toys

_____

_____

_____

Special games

_____

_____

Special books

_____

_____

_____

Dear God,
Thank you for my friends.
Thank you for my toys and special things.
Please teach me to share all I have with others.

Thank you for the world so sweet,
Thank you for the food we eat,
Thank you for the birds that sing,
Thank you God for everything.

Favourite sounds

Favourite colour

Favourite foods

Favourite drinks

Special Things
Use these two pages for your own photographs

My Baptism
My Special Day

Thank you, heavenly Father,
for the family you have given to care for me.
Help them to be loving and patient,
always quick to support and to forgive.
Guide them in all they do
so that their love may show your love,
and the blessing given today
may be with me every day,
keeping me safe from harm,
and helping me to grow up to find purpose
in loving and serving you.

Jesus said to his disciples: 'Go to the people of all nations and make them my disciples. Baptize them in the name of the Father, the Son, and the Holy Spirit… I will be with you always, even until the end of the world.'

Matthew 28:19-20

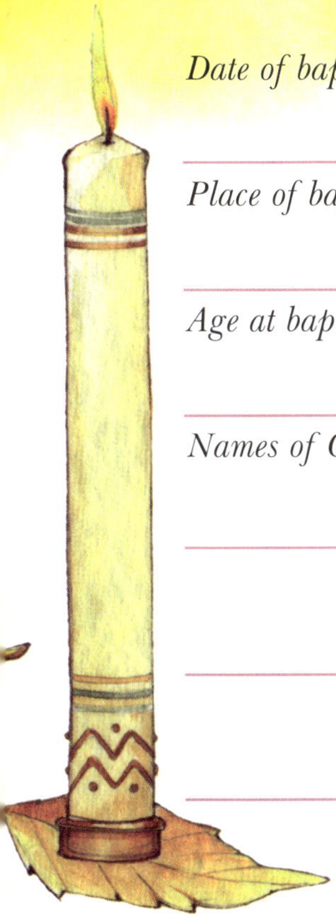

Date of baptism

Place of baptism

Age at baptism

Names of Godparents

Family who attended the service

Friends who attended the service

My Baptism
My Special Day

Use these two pages for your own photographs

My First Christmas

May the joy of the angels,
the wonder of the shepherds,
and the peace of Jesus Christ,
fill our hearts this Christmas time.

[Mary] gave birth to her newborn son. She dressed him in baby clothes and laid him on a bed of hay, because there was no room for them in the inn.

Luke 2:7

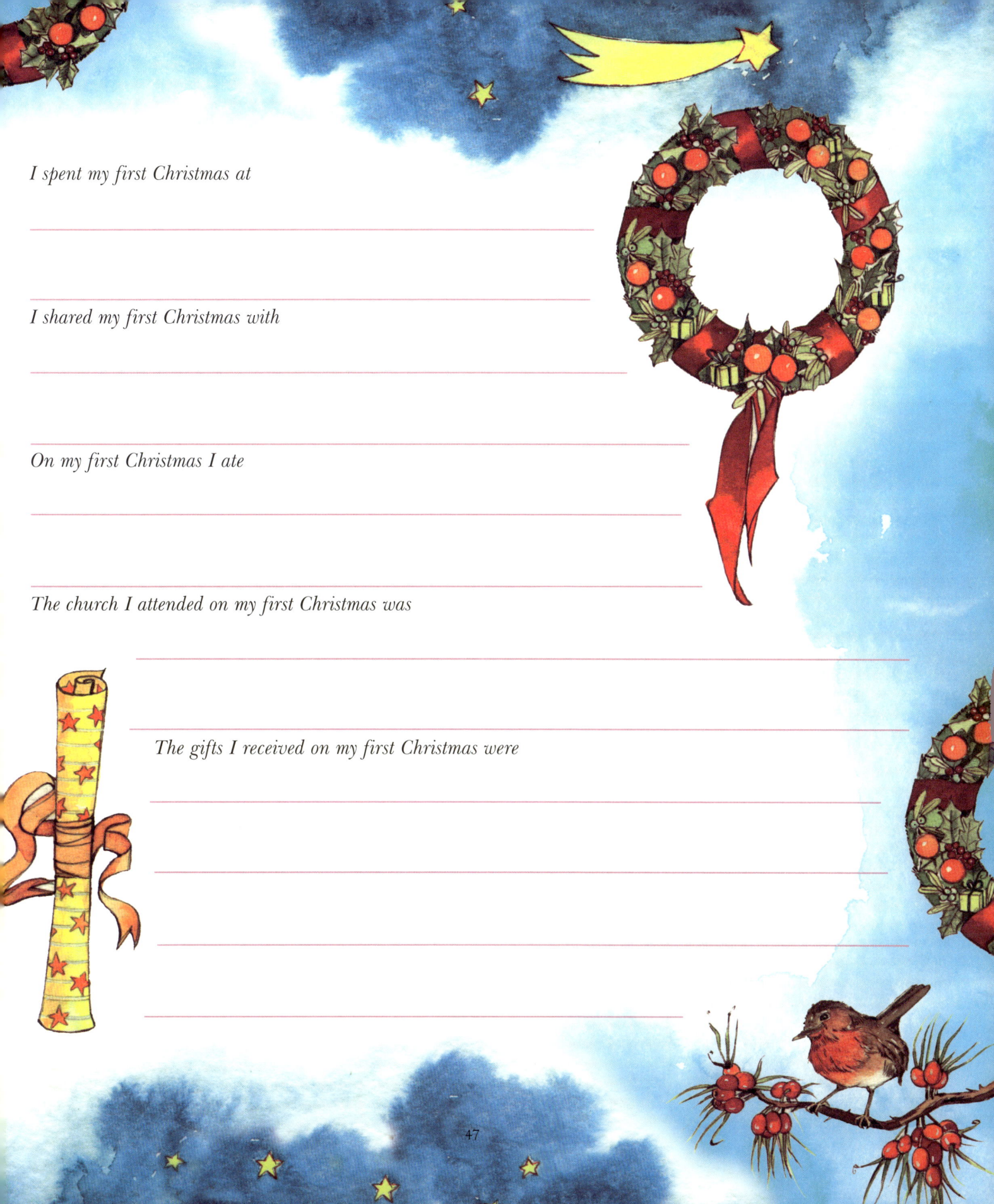

I spent my first Christmas at

I shared my first Christmas with

On my first Christmas I ate

The church I attended on my first Christmas was

The gifts I received on my first Christmas were

My First Christmas
Use these two pages for your own photographs

My First Easter

Thank you, Lord Jesus,
that the sadness of your cruel death
on Good Friday has a happy ending.
Thank you, Lord Jesus,
that you died so my sin could be forgiven.
Thank you, Lord Jesus,
that you rose from the dead
so that I can one day live with you in heaven.
Thank you, Lord Jesus!

Peter said: 'Listen to what I have to say about Jesus from Nazareth... You took him and had evil men put him to death on a cross. But God set him free from death and raised him to life. Death could not hold him in its power.'

Acts 2:22-24

I spent my first Easter at
_____

I shared my first Easter with
_____
_____
_____

On my first Easter I ate
_____
_____

The church I attended on my first Easter was
_____

My First Easter

Use these two pages for your own photographs

Holidays

O God, our Father,
defend us, deliver us, protect us and help us,
as we travel on our journey,
because you are a loving,
caring and compassionate God.

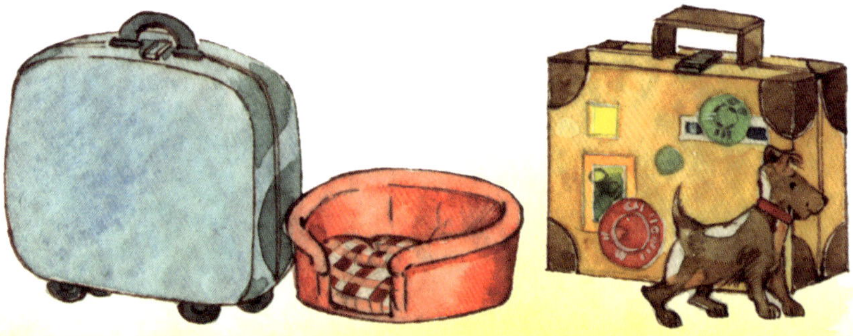

Where I spent my first holiday

Special places I saw and visited

The people I shared my first holiday with

Things I did on my first holiday

Holidays
Use these two pages for your own photographs

My First Birthday

O God, your generous love surrounds us,
and everything we enjoy comes from you.

Dear God, you clothe the lilies of the field,
and feed the birds of the sky.
You lead lambs to pasture and guide deer to water.
Thank you for this special day,
and for all the good gifts you give to us.

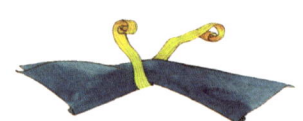

People who came to my party

_____

_____

_____

_____

_____

Special gifts

My First Birthday
Use these two pages for your own photographs